Flip the Flaps
Seashore

Hannah Wilson and Simon Mendez

KINGFISHER

First published 2010 by Kingfisher
This edition published 2012 by Kingfisher
an imprint of Macmillan Children's Books
a division of Macmillan Publishers Limited
20 New Wharf Road, London N1 9RR
Basingstoke and Oxford
Associated companies throughout the world
www.panmacmillan.com

Consultant: David Burnie

ISBN 978-0-7534-3639-4

1 3 5 7 9 8 6 4 2
1TR/0912/UTD/LFA/157MA

A CIP catalogue record for this book is available from the British Library.

Printed in China

Contents

In the rockpool

Many creatures live in rockpools along the seashore. When the tide is out, there may not be much water inside the pool. When the tide is in, the rockpool fills up and bright anemones uncurl their tentacles.

shell

rockpool at low tide

starfish

1. Who lives inside a shell?

2. How does an anemone catch its dinner?

3. Which creatures cling to rocks?

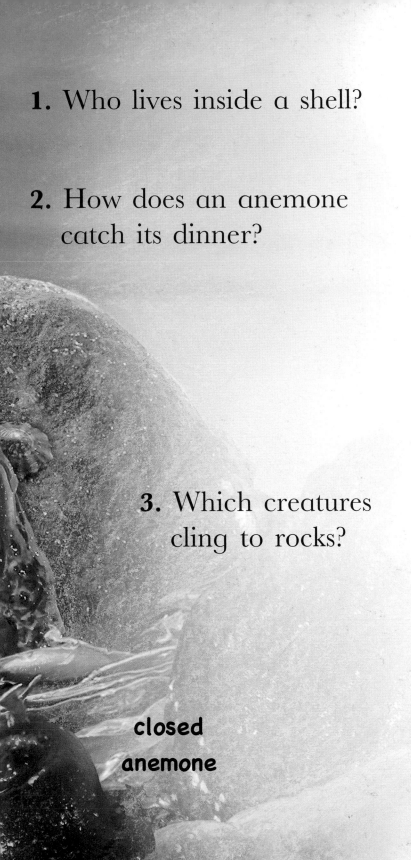

closed
anemone

Creatures that cling to rocks

limpets

barnacles

mussels

5

On the salt marsh

When the sea floods the land, salty marshes can form. Thick with rushes and reeds, they are home to many different birds, including flamingos.

flamingo chick

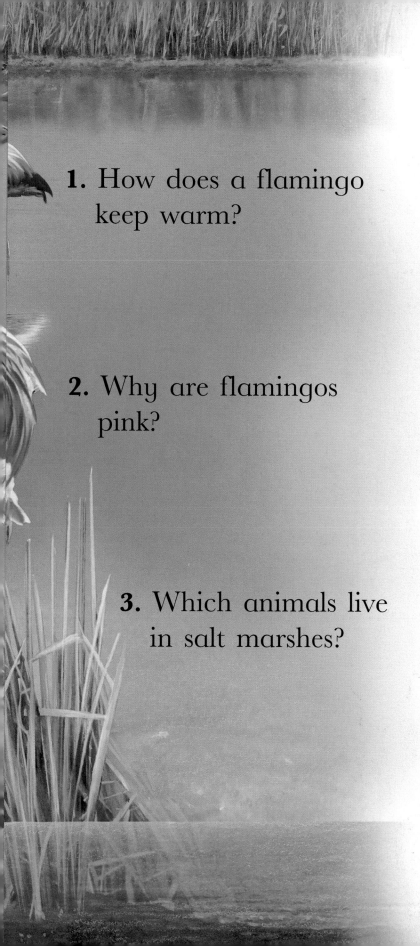

1. How does a flamingo keep warm?

2. Why are flamingos pink?

3. Which animals live in salt marshes?

Other animals on the salt marsh

green-winged teal

dragonfly

Gulf water snake

7

Snowy seashores

In the coldest parts of the
world, animals live by the
sea to hunt for food in its icy
waters. Thick layers of fat,
fur or feathers keep the
animals warm.

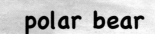

polar bear

male walrus
(a bull)

mother walrus
and her pup

1. Why does a polar bear live on the ice?

2. Which animals have tusks like an elephant and whiskers like a cat?

3. How do penguins splash into the sea?

Penguins like to...

waddle

slide on their stomachs

and dive into the water!

On the beach

When a wave washes up the beach, it drops shells and seaweed onto the sand. The wave also leaves behind tiny creatures for crabs and wading birds to eat.

hungry seagulls

sandcastle

mermaid's purse

crab

hidden starfish

10

1. Why are crabs tricky for seagulls to catch?

2. How many legs does a starfish have?

3. What can you find on the beach?

Things found on the beach

shells

seaweed

jellyfish

Salty swamps

In hot parts of the world,
salty swamps called
mangroves meet the sea.
Filled with plants and trees,
they are home to fish, frogs,
crabs and furry animals
such as monkeys and otters.

fishing
cat

long-tailed
macaque monkeys

1. Do monkeys swim in the sea?

2. How does a fishing cat catch fish?

3. How do smooth-coated otters look after their babies?

Looking after baby otters

mother and father otters

otter pups outside burrow

learning to swim

Rocky islands

Many seashore animals live
on islands far out at sea.
They have their babies on
land, among the rocks and
cliffs, but dive deep into
the ocean to find food.

iguanas
sunbathing

14

1. Which lizards live by the sea?

2. Why are some marine iguanas pink and white?

3. Where do puffins make their nests?

How puffins live on cliffs

mother and baby chick

inside a burrow

diving for fish

Night-time on the beach

The seashore can be safer for some animals at night. Predators (animals that hunt other animals) find it hard to hunt in the darkness. Bats, however, are excellent night-time hunters.

loggerhead turtle

1. A turtle likes to [lay] eggs in a sandy [spot] on a beach.

2. The turtle lays [up to] 100 eggs. They [are] like ping-pong [balls].

laying egg[s]

3. A fisherman ba[t flies] at night. It flies [over] the beach and [scoops] up fish with its [feet].

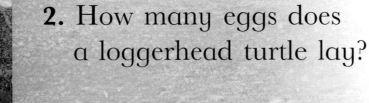

1. Why does a turtle like the beach?

2. How many eggs does a loggerhead turtle lay?

3. Which 'fisherman' hunts at night?

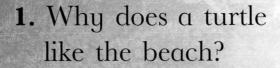
[fisherm]an bat hunts

[ac]ross water

[scoops] up a fish

17

Index